Level 2 is ideal [for children who have] received
some reading instruction[. They can read]
simple sentences with help.

Special features:

Frequent repetition of main
story words and phrases

Short,
simple
sentences

The king took the girl to a
room full of straw.

"You must spin this straw
into gold," the king said.

The girl began to cry.
"I cannot do this," she said.

Large,
clear type

A funny little man came
into the room.

"If you give me your
necklace, I will help you,"
said the man.

"Yes," said the girl. "I will
give you my necklace."

Careful match
between
story and
pictures

Educational Consultant:
Geraldine Taylor

A catalogue record for this book is available from the British Library

Published by Ladybird Books Ltd
80 Strand, London, WC2R 0RL
A Penguin Company

001 - 10 9 8 7 6 5 4 3 2 1
© LADYBIRD BOOKS LTD MMXI
Ladybird, Read It Yourself and the Ladybird Logo are registered or
unregistered trade marks of Ladybird Books Limited.

ISBN: 978-1-40930-713-6

Printed in China

Rumpelstiltskin

Illustrated by Marina Le Ray

One day, a poor man took his daughter to see the king.

"My daughter can spin straw into gold," said the poor man.

The king took the girl to a
room full of straw.

"You must spin this straw
into gold," the king said.

The girl began to cry.
"I cannot do this," she said.

A funny little man came into the room.

"If you give me your necklace, I will help you," said the man.

"Yes," said the girl. "I will give you my necklace."

The next day, the room was full of gold.

So the king gave the girl more straw to spin into gol

The funny little man came into the room.

"If you give me your ring, I will help you," said the funny little man.

"Yes," said the girl. "I will give you my ring."

The next day the room was full of gold.

The king gave the girl more straw. "If you can spin this straw into gold," he said, "you will be my queen."

The funny little man came into the room.

"If you give me your first child, I will help you," said the funny little man.

"Yes," said the girl. "I will give you my first child."

The next day the room was full of gold.

The king married the girl. Soon, they had a child.

The funny little man came to see the queen.

"If you cannot guess my name," said the man, "you must give me your child."

The queen began to cry.

The queen sent her men to find every name they could.

But she could not guess the name of the funny little man.

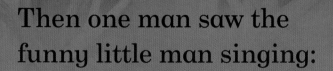

Then one man saw the
funny little man singing:

"The queen will never win my game,

For Rumpelstiltskin is my name!"

The man went to tell
the queen.

The next day the queen said to the funny little man, "Is your name... Rumpelstiltskin?"

And the funny little man was so cross, he ran away and was never seen again.

How much do you remember about
the story of Rumpelstiltskin? Answer
these questions and find out!

- What did the poor man
  say the girl could do?

- Who helped her to
  do this?

- Can you name two
  things the girl gave
  the funny little man?

- How did the queen find
  out Rumpelstiltskin's
  name?